ECONOMICS

mpany

10/06

DEMCO

This book owes much to Peter R. Liverakos and Susan M. Shwartz, who toil in the fiscal wilderness on a daily basis.

Lerner Publications Company
A division of Lerner Publishing Group
241 First Avenue North
Minneapolis, MN 55401 U.S.A.

Website address: www.lernerbooks.com

Library of Congress Cataloging-in-Publication Data

Gilman, Laura Anne.
　　Economics / by Laura Anne Gilman.
　　　　p.　cm. — (How economics works)
　　Includes bibliographical references and index.
　　ISBN-13: 978–0–8225–2662–9 (lib. bdg. : alk. paper)
　　ISBN-10: 0–8225–2662–X (lib. bdg. : alk. paper)
　　1. Economics—Juvenile literature. I. Title. II. Series.
　　HB183.G55　2006
　　330—dc22　　　　　　　　　　　　2005009042

Manufactured in the United States of America
1 2 3 4 5 6 – DP – 11 10 09 08 07 06

TABLE OF CONTENTS

CHAPTER 1
WHY SHOULD I CARE?

Economics is all about money, finances, markets, and other words you might hear your parents talking about at the dinner table or while they're watching the evening news. It's also the study of how money acts and reacts, not only in the United States but all over the world. Economics is the study of money on a large scale—the stock market and world currencies, for example.

You might think economics is something kids don't need to think about, because it doesn't affect them. But economics isn't something that's way out there in the distance. It's in your front yard and in your house. It influences and changes how you live. For example, our standard of living—the quality and quantity of our goods and services (things and helpful acts that can be bought or sold) is measured by how well the economy is doing.

MONEY TALK The word *economy* can be traced back to the Greek word *oikonomos*, "one who manages a household," which comes from *oikos*, "house," and *nemein*, "to manage."

Maybe, like a lot of American families, one of your parents has lost a job because the boss needed to cut costs. Or you haven't been able to get more allowance, because—and here's the important phrase—the economy's so bad. In this book, you'll see how economics affects our lives. And you'll also see how we affect the economy through the choices we make every single day.

Okay, so what? I don't have a job yet. Why do I have to bother with the economy?

You don't. But don't think the economy doesn't know about you. Believe it or not, kids your age are major players in the economy. The economy influences what you do and what you buy, the college you can afford to go to, the job you get when you're out of school, and the place you will live. And you, in turn, influence the economy by

MONEY TALK Economists (people who study economics) who specialize in microeconomics study the activity of individual producers and consumers rather than the economy as a whole.

the choices you make in spending and managing your own money. In other words, you are the economy—or at least one small but important part of it. Don't believe it? Just watch some television. Count the number of ads that are either selling something to you or use kids in the commercial to sell something to your parents. You're a consumer. And the economy is based on getting consumers to consume—to spend the money they earn.

You influence the economy when you spend money on your favorite toys. Tweens (children between 8 and 12 years old) are one of the most powerful consumer groups. They spend billions of dollars each year.

Say, for example, you want a bicycle—or the newest electronic game—for your birthday. If the economy is good and your parents' jobs are secure, they may have enough available income (money) to buy exactly what you want. If the economy is bad, however, your parents' jobs might be uncertain. Then they may not be able to afford the gift you want. Not because they don't love you but because they have bills—rent or mortgage (money paid for shelter), groceries, electricity, car payments, dentist or doctor bills, and taxes. These must be paid before they can spend money on anything else.

NEEDS AND WANTS

All these bills pay for needs—the items and services that people must have to live safe, healthy lives. Bicycles and electronic games are wants. Wants are things and services we would like to have but don't need in order to live.

Let's take a closer look at wants, such as your bicycle. When people have plenty of money, they want to buy bicycles. This creates a high demand for bicycles. Factories need to make more bicycles so stores can sell them. To supply more bicycles, the bicycle-making factories will need to hire more workers. The people who are hired earn money and receive paychecks. They buy things with their money, creating a demand for more goods. To meet the demand for more goods, more people are hired to produce these goods. These workers may be able to buy some wants in addition to paying for their needs. That's a healthy economy.

If the economy isn't healthy, people can't afford to buy wants, such as bicycles. The bicycle-making factory won't make so many bikes, because people can't afford to buy them. The factory also won't need so many workers because people aren't buying many bicycles. The bicycle factory will lay off some of its workers. Those workers lose their jobs. Without jobs, they will have no money to buy their needs, such as food, or their wants. The flow of money—the way money flows in payment from businesses to workers, then back to businesses as workers buy goods and services—is slowed down or stopped. That's an unhealthy economy.

Okay, you're saying. I get it now. But how is understanding any of this going to help me? This book

BOTTOM LINE "It's the economy, stupid!" was Bill Clinton's unofficial election motto during the 1992 U.S. presidential campaign between Clinton and President George H. W. Bush. The motto referred to Bush's problems dealing with the nation's bad economy and high unemployment. Many people think Bush lost the election because of these problems.

This factory in Flint, Michigan, was shut down in the late 1980s because of the poor economy at the time.

can give you the information you need to make decisions that are right for you.

LEARNING THE LINGO

Okay, so learning about the way the economy works won't mean that you'll always have money to spend. It won't magically increase your allowance or make your birthday checks larger. But you will understand the terms people use when they talk about the economy—words like *inflation*, *supply and demand*, and *debt*.

Adam Smith (1723–1790) is known as the founder of modern economics. He was a Scottish philosopher and economist best known for his book *The Wealth of Nations*, published in 1776.

Then you will also understand the interesting and important ideas they're talking about.

That means you won't have to wait for someone else to tell you what's going on. You'll be able to follow what your parents are discussing at the dinner table, what your teachers are talking about in class, and what the newscasters are reporting on the news. Remember, economics isn't limited to specialists. Anyone can play. All you have to do is know the rules.

Chapter 2
Money Makes the World Go 'Round

Before we start talking about your role in the economy, it would help to take a look at the big picture. Every country has its own economy, with its own rules and specific ways of doing things. In fact, economies are a little bit like families. For example, your family's way of handling chores is probably different from the way your best friend's family does chores. One way may seem to make more sense to you than the other, even though

You can create an economic system based on your family chores. Decide how much each chore would be worth, depending on how important it is to the family and how much skill it takes to perform.

there are many ways to do chores. Just as different families have different ideas about doing chores, different governments have their own ideas on how to run the economy. Most countries follow one of two economic plans, or models. One model is called free enterprise and is based on capitalist ideas. The other plan is called central planning and is based on Communist or Socialist ideas.

CAPITALISM

In the United States, we have a capitalist economy, also called the free market system or free enterprise. Most Western nations (the United States, Canada, and the

VALUE ADDED

The European Union (EU) is a group of European countries that work together for peace and prosperity. The countries vote to decide important matters. The EU works to increase economic growth among its members. The European Union began with six countries—Belgium, Germany, France, Italy, Luxembourg, and the Netherlands. By 2005 it had twenty-five member countries, and more countries apply for membership every year.

European Union) and Japan are based on a free market or capitalist system.

In this system, individuals and private businesses own factories and businesses, produce goods, provide services, and compete with each other for customers. The government influences this system. The government passes laws that give companies certain rules they must follow. For example, the U.S. government regulates (sets rules for) health and safety conditions in certain businesses, such as meatpacking. Meatpackers prepare meat for transportation and sale.

Sometimes a government will decide to deregulate, or stop setting rules for, the way a company does business. For example, for many years, the U.S. government regulated how U.S. airlines set prices for tickets. In the 1980s, the government decided to allow the airlines to set their own prices for tickets.

In a free enterprise, or capitalist, economy, businesses often compete with each other. They have large sales or set their prices lower than a competitor who offers the same goods or services.

CENTRAL PLANNING

In a centrally planned economy, the government controls everything. The government owns the businesses, the buildings, the land the buildings sit on, and the machinery used for production. The government also decides who will work at each business, how long the employees will work, and the amount of money they will earn. The government also controls who may sell those products and the price that can be charged for them.

The most familiar example of this type of economy is probably the former Soviet Union (1922–1991) and China. However, in the twenty-first century, China and the nations of the former Soviet Union allow more privately owned businesses to operate.

In Israel some people choose to live on small farms, called kibbutzim. Everyone in the kibbutz shares equally in the work—whether farming, cooking, or child care. Every member of the

MONEY Makers Karl Marx (1818–1883) was one of the most important German thinkers of the 1800s. He wrote *The Communist Manifesto* in 1848 with his friend Friedrich Engels. Marx later wrote *Das Kapital*.

In his books, Marx explained the theory of Communism and discussed his other ideas about economics.

A kibbutz is its own economic system. On this kibbutz in Israel, workers grow apples.

kibbutz shares what is produced. The Israeli government does not have central control of the system. People volunteer to take part in the system. It is a good example of a healthy, Socialist economic system, in which people give according to their abilities and receive according to their needs.

In the twenty-first century, many countries mix and match free enterprise with government regulation to create a system that works for them. For most nations, that is a mix of private ownership and some government control.

No Money? No Problem!

You probably already know about a third kind of economy. It's called the barter system. Barter is the exchange of one product or service for another. When you trade something from your lunch for something from a friend's lunch, you're bartering. Or if you walk your neighbor's dog in exchange for homemade brownies, you're bartering. In a barter economy, no money changes hands. Bartering was common in the early part of American history, when England ruled much of North America. American colonists (settlers) bartered among themselves and with Native Americans. Colonists often used wampum, beads made from shells, to trade with Native Americans. But on a large scale, bartering isn't very practical. Imagine having to exchange one thousand pounds of flour for one thousand cows! Money is a much easier way to pay for goods and services.

The barter system is a very old economic system and can work very well on a small scale.

A Global Economy

People travel from one country to another all the time. Cars built in one country are shipped to another country, where they are sold to consumers there. The same is true of the sneakers you're wearing or the television you watch. These items were probably made in a faraway country. They were shipped to the United States, where you and your family bought them. And just as the items move around, so too does the money that pays for them. We live in a global economy.

Most nations count on world trade to improve their economies. One nation may need a resource that it does not have or does not have enough of. For example, the United States depends on Middle Eastern countries to get the oil it needs. But sometimes nations try to limit trade with other nations. They put a tariff, or tax, on goods that come from other countries. This tax makes the imported products more expensive than those made in the home country. Nations can also set quotas, or a limit, on the amount of imported goods that come into a country.

The Internet makes it very easy for people in one country to buy and sell things with people in another country without ever leaving home. Using a computer, a buyer

Purchasing goods online is an easy way to participate in the global economy. Remember, get your parents' permission before buying anything online!

here in the United States can purchase something from a British website, for example. Or if you can understand a foreign language, you can shop at online stores in France, Italy, Japan, or almost anywhere in the world. You pay for whatever you buy with a credit card. You pay in dollars. But the merchant at the other end receives euros (in most of Europe), yen (in Japan), the British pound in Great Britain, or whatever currency the merchant prefers.

BANK ON IT Canada, Mexico, and the United States signed the North American Free Trade Agreement (NAFTA) in 1992. The agreement went into effect on January 1, 1994. It made trade among these three countries less expensive and easier by getting rid of tariffs on goods made and sold in North America.

CHAPTER 3
THE RULES OF THE GAME

When you hear the word *market,* you may think of your local supermarket or a farmers market. You would not be wrong. A market can be a physical place where people can exchange goods or services for money. But a market can also be a worldwide stock market. In a stock market, people buy and sell shares of stock. Shares are part ownership of a business. People who do business on the stock market may never see each other. They conduct business by using telephones, fax machines, and computers. Markets are where all the action happens in the economy.

I WANT. YOU GOT?

Most markets are driven by supply and demand. Supply is how much of a product there is. Demand refers to how many people want the product. Remember the excitement around the holidays when a hot new toy comes to the stores? People line up outside the stores before they've even opened. If people miss their chance to buy the hot, new item, they're willing to go on e-bay and pay even more than it cost in the store. They think they have to have this wonderful, new thing. Watch that happen once or twice, and you'll understand supply and demand.

A crowd of shoppers wait for a toy store to open for business in New York City.

You know that supply is the amount of a product that a company is willing and able to produce. Demand is the amount of a product that consumers want to buy. Ideally, there is an equal supply for every demand. In a perfectly balanced economic world, there's a pumpkin at Halloween for everyone who wants to buy one. But what happens if there's a drought—a long period of dry weather without rain? Or a pumpkin-

eating bug destroys the harvest? Then there may not be a pumpkin for every pumpkin buyer. With few pumpkins for sale, pumpkins become a scarcity, or a scarce resource.

Let's look at that pumpkin shortage again. A lot of jack-o'-lantern makers want a pumpkin. What's more, they want a nice, round, healthy pumpkin that will look good when it's

carved. But of the one hundred pumpkins the market has for sale, only twenty of them are A-quality pumpkins—big and round and good for carving. Another thirty of them are B-quality. They're smaller but still good for carving. Thirty more are too small for carving. You'd have to draw the jack-o'-lantern face on those pumpkins. The last twenty are rotten, so nobody will want them.

So which kind of pumpkin would you buy? The A-quality pumpkin, of course. And the person selling the pumpkins knows that. Sellers can charge more for the A-quality pumpkins because there usually aren't enough for everyone who wants one. The supply of pumpkins is not meeting the demand.

COMPETITION

It might seem as though the pumpkin seller could charge any price for the A-quality pumpkins. But if the price of those pumpkins gets too high, buyers can go down the road to see if another market has them for a better price. That's called competition. Maybe the market down the road is selling its best pumpkins for two dollars less. That's where the smart customer will go.

Which seller will earn the most money? The market that sells pumpkins for less money earns less per pumpkin. But that seller is likely to sell all its A-quality pumpkins. The more expensive pumpkin seller will make more money per

pumpkin, but he or she might not sell all the pumpkins. The less expensive pumpkin seller makes more money overall.

What if the government steps in and says that pumpkins must be priced according to a certain set of standards (size, color, shape, freshness)? That brings us back to regulation. Then the pumpkin market would be regulated. Only pumpkins that were a certain size, a certain shape, and just the right shade of orange would qualify as A-quality pumpkins. What would happen if the government regulated how many pumpkins could be sold? How would that affect the price of pumpkins? If the demand for pumpkins was greater than the supply, the price would probably go up. The demand would be greater than the supply. If supply was greater than the demand, the price would probably go down.

WHAT'S A SERVICE?

People don't only buy things, or goods, in the market. They also buy services. A service is an act that one person or group (a company or a government) does for another person or group for a fee. If your parents have someone come in to clean the house every week, that's

Shoveling snow for money is a service.

a service that your parents pay for. When your neighbors pay you to shovel the walkway, you're providing a service for them.

What if it snowed heavily and all the neighbors want their walks shoveled? If only a few kids in the neighborhood are willing to do the job, shoveling is a service that is scarce. The kids with shovels can charge a higher price than if a lot of people were competing for the jobs.

Remember the pumpkin example? This time, it's not goods, or products, that are scarce but a service. Because the demand is high and the service is scarce, the cost of the service increases. If the price of the service, like the price of the pumpkins, becomes too high, people may decide to shovel their own walks. Or kids from another neighborhood might offer their service for a lower price. Businesses, whether small or large, almost always have competition—someone who will offer the same or a similar product or service for less money.

BEHIND THE SCENES

Not all buying and selling of goods and services takes place right in front of your eyes. A lot of buying and selling takes place behind the scenes—way before you buy a product in a store. For example, a farmer who grows wheat sells it to a mill. After it is ground into flour, it is sold to bakers, who make the bread that you buy to make a sandwich. You never see the farmer or the miller, but they are necessary for you to get your bread. Buying and selling goods and services take place at each step of the bread-making process.

BANK ON IT What is the gross domestic product (GDP)? The GDP is a measure of the total value of all the goods and services produced within a country during a certain amount of time (usually one year).

Here's another example, right in your hands. Books are made from paper. Paper comes from wood pulp, which comes from trees. Trees are grown as a crop (product), much the same way wheat is. Loggers cut the trees down (a service). Mills buy the logs to make wood pulp, the fibers used to make paper. Then the paper manufacturers buy the wood pulp to make paper (another product). Printing companies buy paper to print on. Printers send book pages to a bindery, where they are bound (another service) into books. Booksellers buy the books (products) to sell to their customers. Sometimes it's a long chain between the original resource (trees) and you, the final consumer.

IT'S JUST REAL-LIFE MONOPOLY!

In his book *Everything I Need to Know about Business I Learned from Monopoly*, Alan Axelrod suggests that the rules of the game Monopoly can be used to succeed in the business world. This applies to economics too. Everything you need to know about business you've already learned if you've ever played Monopoly.

Challenge your parents or siblings to a game of Monopoly. Keep track of what does and doesn't work in terms of strategy. Set a time limit to keep things moving.

Think about it. You buy property (real estate) and improve it by building houses or hotels. But you have to pay to have those hotels put up. Then, if someone lands on your property, you collect rent. If you land on utility squares, you have to pay for electricity, gas, and phone service. And if you land on a railroad square that another player owns, you must pay for the transportation service they're providing. It's just a game, but the game looks a lot like the economy in action. The basics are the same.

CHAPTER 4
PLAY THE GAME

People have to make economic choices. Do you want to spend your money to go out to a movie or for burgers? Do you want that new CD or a new pair of shoes? Governments, too, must decide how to spend money. Do they have enough money to build new roads, fix old bridges, and buy more tanks for the army? Individuals and governments all have to ask: is it more important to meet immediate needs and wants or to save and plan for the future? In a healthy economy, most people and governments try to do both.

A GROWING ECONOMY

A healthy economy is one that grows. It raises our standard of living. That means that the economy produces more and better goods and services. But what makes an economy grow? How does it produce more and better goods and services? A healthy, growing economy needs natural resources (such as water and soil), capital (factories, equipment, money), a labor force (workers), and technology (research and inventions). These things are called productive resources. Working together, they produce more and better goods and services, which raises the standard of living.

A healthy economy works like this. A nation combines its productive resources to build new factories. The factories buy equipment that has the best new technology.

THE PATTERN OF THE ECONOMY

People

Money spent for goods and services

Wages, salaries and profits earned producing goods and services

Business and industry

The factory managers hire workers and train them to use the new equipment. With the high-tech equipment, the workers are more productive. They produce more goods in less time, with less effort, and fewer materials.

How It Works

People grow up learning different skills and information. Some people learn how to use machinery to make things in a factory. They produce goods, such as cars or clothing. Some people work in offices or stores or banks or hospitals or fire stations. They mainly provide services. Whatever workers do, they get paid for their work. They use their pay to buy other goods and services, such as food, housing, or a trip to Disneyland. Some of their pay

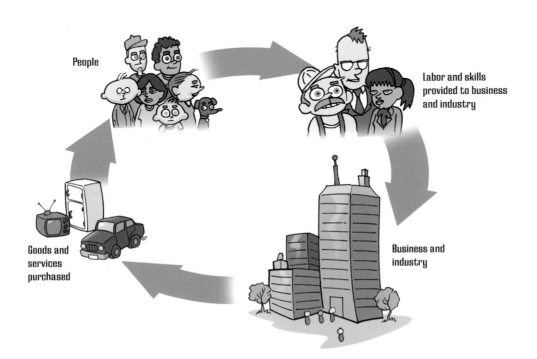

People

Labor and skills provided to business and industry

Business and industry

Goods and services purchased

goes back to other businesses. Those businesses use the money they make to pay their own workers. Those workers use their pay to buy more goods and services.

In a healthy economy, this system works well. But sometimes businesses fail. With no money to pay workers, the owner of a failing business must lay off workers. The workers can't afford to buy all the goods and services they want or need. So the businesses that once served the laid-off workers sell fewer goods and services. Maybe they, too, will have to lay off some workers, which affects other businesses and workers.

MONEY Makers Alan Greenspan (born in 1926) is the chairman of the Federal Reserve Board. He is one of the most important people in the world, because what he says about the economy influences economic decisions around the globe.

When demand for goods and services drops, production drops. Income and employment drop even more. When a nation's business activity slumps, the economy goes into a recession, a period of low economic activity. If many businesses across the country close and millions of people are out of work for a very long time, the economy goes into a depression. In the United States, severe depressions occurred in 1837, 1873, 1893, and 1907. The worst depression in all history, called the Great Depression, began in 1929 and lasted until the early 1940s. Recessions still happen in the United States and around the world. But in the United States, the government usually takes measures to help the economy before a recession leads to a depression.

THE GREAT DEPRESSION

In October 1929, people realized they were paying too much for stocks. All at once, thousands of people tried to sell their stocks. With so many sellers and not enough buyers, stock prices fell. On Tuesday, October 29, 1929, the New York Stock Exchange crashed. Stock that had been worth thousands of dollars was suddenly worthless. That event marked the beginning of the Great Depression in the United States and throughout the world. Factories, banks, and stores closed, businesses collapsed, and many farmers lost their farms because they could not pay the mortgage. Many people who lost their jobs also lost their homes. When the banks closed, people often lost their life's savings. About one-third of the country's workers were out of work by 1932.

Homeless people lived in rough shacks made from scraps of wood and metal. Groups of shacks were called Hoovervilles, named after President Herbert Hoover. He was president when the Depression struck. Men, women, and children stood in bread lines *(right)*, run by welfare agencies and religious groups, to get something to eat. People ate scraps of food they found in garbage cans. Many died of disease from malnutrition.

When Franklin D. Roosevelt became president in 1933, Americans got help. Roosevelt started many government programs (called the New Deal) to get people working once again. In the United States, the Great Depression ended when the country entered World War II (1939–1945). U.S. factories grew and hired many workers to produce war materials for the U.S. armed forces. The Great Depression was the longest period of economic depression the country has known.

During an economic boom, employment and production rise rapidly. Usually, consumer demand rises during boom periods. Sometimes companies can't produce enough goods and services to meet the demand. When the supply does not keep up with the demand, inflation (rapidly rising prices) can occur. When inflation becomes extreme, people cannot afford to buy the goods and services they need.

In the end, all the talk about the economy comes down to a simple formula. Needs and wants create economic action. People purchase goods and services. The demand for goods and services, in turn, creates jobs. Jobs generate income for workers, who then have money to spend. The money they spend helps businesses grow to create newer and more products. Consumers want these products. This cycle repeats itself, raising the standard of living.

MONEY TALK The U.S. Department of Labor tracks the consumer price index (CPI) month by month. The CPI measures the changes in the price of goods and services bought by most people in the United States. The CPI compares the existing price of certain goods and services with their cost at an earlier period of time. It is used to measure the rate of inflation, a continual increase in the price of goods and services throughout the nation's economy.

CHAPTER 5
MAKING IT WORK FOR YOU

You are a part of the economy. You decide how to spend your allowance, and you may sway your parents' decision about what kind of television or computer to buy. Later on in your life, as part of the labor force, you will earn a regular paycheck yourself. But what if you think economics is actually pretty interesting. What then?

Look at the options around you. Your school may not offer business or economics classes, but there are plenty of ways to increase your own education. Earn

business-related badges in the Scouts. Take a class at your local Y or community center. Don't let anyone say you're too young to learn this stuff. Age isn't important. Interest is what counts most.

When you're in high school and college, you'll have many choices about what you want to study. You might like to learn more about the basic principles of economics. Or you might find that you're more interested in the nuts and bolts of business. You may decide that a firm grounding in the basics of economics is all you want. If so, you'll still be ahead of most people. You may want to major in economics.

And if you do, what then? What sorts of jobs are available?

Economics teachers may specialize in many subjects, from economic theory to public finance to banking to international trade.

SHARE THE WEALTH

One choice is to become an economics teacher—either in high school or college. You can teach other young economists or do research. Or you might choose to become an economist yourself, and come up with new ideas to explain what is happening in the world's economies and why.

MAKING MONEY BY MAKING MONEY

Another job choice is to work as a broker in the stock exchange. The stock exchange is a marketplace for buying and selling stocks and bonds. Owning stocks means that you own

BOTTOM LINE An economist is a man who states the obvious in terms of the incomprehensible [something that's impossible to understand].
—Alfred A. Knopf (1892–1984), a leading U.S. book publisher

shares, or parts, of a company. People who own stocks are called shareholders. Brokers represent shareholders who want to buy or sell stocks and bonds. Bonds are certificates issued by the government or by a business for money loaned. They are promises that the government or the business will pay back the borrowed money plus interest. Brokers do the actual buying and selling. The broker tells the buyer or seller what the price of the stock is that day. If the shareholder still wants to buy or sell stock, the

MONEY TALK The Securities and Exchange Commission (SEC) is a U.S. government agency that makes and enforces laws about buying and selling stocks and bonds.

A stock ticker display on Wall Street in New York City shows sales of stocks. The letters on a stock ticker are called stock symbols and represent stock-holding companies.

broker sends the order to the stock exchange. This is usually done electronically with computers.

COUNTING MONEY

Maybe you have an eye for detail and really like math. A certified public accountant (CPA) prepares and checks the financial records of companies and individuals. A company's financial statement tells the shareholder whether the company's stock is gaining or losing value. CPAs are gatekeepers. They make sure that everything on the financial statement is clear and correct before it is sent to the shareholder. Certified public accountants must pass the Uniform CPA Examination and get a special license to qualify as a CPA. Certified public accountants can work for big companies, government agencies, or as individuals in business for themselves.

BANK ON IT

You might also consider working for a bank. Banks offer many different jobs—from tellers (the people who handle deposits and withdrawals) to loan officers. Loan officers help

Loan officers help people take out loans for many things, from a new house to a new car to college.

people apply for loans. A loan officer decides how big a risk the bank will take if it makes the loan. Will the people be able to repay the money they borrowed? If not, they won't get a loan.

OTHER CHOICES

Economists have all sorts of different job opportunities. And they work in many different fields in both business and government. Labor economists, for example, study wages, hours worked, and laws regarding labor. Agricultural economists study the costs of running a farm. Industrial economists study the costs of running companies. They look at the cost of producing a product and study the market for that product to see if it will sell.

Or you might be interested in international trade—how and why countries buy and sell things to each other. Other economists study health and insurance issues. Maybe you'll want to work for the Congressional Budget Office (CBO) in Washington, D.C. The CBO gives information about the U.S. economy to members of Congress. All sorts of opportunities exist. See what appeals to you.

MONEY Makers John Maynard Keynes (1883–1946) was a British economist who revolutionized the field of economics. He created something called macroeconomics, the study of economics on a large scale. His book *The General Theory of Employment, Interest and Money* was published in 1936. It is one of the most important books on economics.

GLOSSARY

bond: a certificate issued by the government or by a business for money loaned

broker: a person who helps people buy or sell stocks and bonds

competition: two or more sellers working to get the business of buyers by offering the lowest price for their goods or services

debt: something owed; owing money for something received

demand: the amount of a product that consumers want to buy

depression: a long period of time when a nation's business slows down and many people lose their jobs

economic growth: an increase in the goods and services produced by a country over a certain period of time

finance: managing money matters

goods: a physical item, such as food or shoes, that can be bought or sold

income: money that is received in the form of wages, salary, rent, interest, profit, or gifts

inflation: a general increase in the price of goods and services

macroeconomics: the study of economics on a large (country-sized) scale, including a nation's total production, employment, and prices

market: a meeting of people who want to buy and sell goods and services either directly or through other people. In large markets, such as the stock market, buyers and sellers often buy and sell by telephone, fax machines, and computers.

microeconomics: the study of individual producers and consumers

recession: a period of slowed business activity. Production, buying, selling, and employment are lower than usual but not as bad as in a depression.

services: useful acts, such as hauling away garbage, that can be bought or sold

shareholders: people who own stock in a company

stock: a piece of paper that shows that you own shares, or parts, of a company

stock exchange: a marketplace for buying and selling stocks and bonds

supply: the amount of a product that is available to buy

tariff: a tax on imported (incoming) or exported (outgoing) goods

BIBLIOGRAPHY

Axelrod, Alan. *Everything I Need to Know about Business I Learned from Monopoly.* Philadelphia: Running Press, 2002.

Godfrey, Neale S. *Neale S. Godfrey's Ultimate Kids' Money Book.* New York: Simon & Schuster, 1998.

Sowell, Thomas. *Basic Economics: A Citizen's Guide to the Economy.* New York: Basic Books, 2000.

FURTHER READING

Drew, Bonnie. *Money Skills: 101 Activities to Teach Your Child about Money.* Hawthorne, NJ: The Career Press, 1992.

Fuller, Donna Jo. *The Stock Market.* Minneapolis: Lerner Publications Company, 2006.

Harman, Hollis Page. *Barron's Money Sense for Kids!* Hauppauge, NY: Barron's Educational Series, Inc., 2004.

Maybury, Richard J. *Whatever Happened to Penny Candy?* Placerville, CA: Bluestocking Press, 1993.

Thomas, Keltie. *The Kids Guide to Money Cents.* Tonawanda, NY: Kids Can Press Ltd., 2004.

WEBSITES

Headbone Zone
> http://www.headbone.com/wtvrags/
> In this rags-to-riches game, you'll plan, organize, and run a ten-city concert tour for the band Groovy Gravy. Apply economic principles as you decide on ticket prices and set up a budget for advertising.

Lava Mind
> http://www.gazillionaire.com/gaz.html
> This is an intergalactic game of business strategy—Monopoly in outer space.

National Council on Economic Education (NCEE) Online
http://www.nationalcouncil.org
This is the site of the National Council on Economic Education (NCEE). The council is a nationwide network that promotes economic literacy. Its mission is to help students develop the real-life skills they need to think and choose responsibly as consumers, savers, investors, members of the workforce, and participants in a global economy.

INDEX

About the Author

Laura Anne Gilman is a freelance writer and editor. She is the author of *Coping with Cerebral Palsy* and *Yeti: The Abominable Snowman,* as well as the fantasy trilogy Grail Quest. She lives in northern New Jersey and can be found on the Web at http://www.sff.net/people/lauraanne.gilman.

Photo Acknowledgments

The images in this book are used with the permission of: Bill Hauser, pp. 1, 4, 7, 11, 20, 22, 23, 24, 29, 30–31, 35, 36, 39; © Hypnoclips, pp. 5 (both), 8, 19, 26, 34, 37 (bottom), 38 (top); © Palmer/Kane/CORBIS, p. 6; © Bob Krist/ CORBIS, p. 9; © SuperStock, Inc./SuperStock, p. 10; © RubberBall/ SuperStock, p. 12; © age footstock/SuperStock, pp. 14, 37 (top), 38 (bottom); © Richard T. Nowitz/CORBIS, p. 15; © Charles Gupton/CORBIS, p. 17; © Paul Barton/CORBIS, p. 18; © Lynn Goldsmith/CORBIS, p. 21; © George Glod/SuperStock, p. 25; © David Forbert/SuperStock, p. 27; © Culver Pictures, Inc./ SuperStock, p. 33; © Ariel Skelley/CORBIS, p. 40.

Front cover: Bill Hauser. Back cover: © Hypnoclips (both)